Interference Effects

Claire Dyer holds a BA in English & History from the University of Birmingham, an MA in Victorian Literature & Culture from the University of Reading and an MA in Creative Writing from Royal Holloway, University of London. She lives in Reading, Berkshire.

By the same author:

Poetry
   Eleven Rooms, Two Rivers Press (2013)

Fiction
   The Moment, Quercus (2013)
   Falling for Gatsby, Quercus (2014)
   The Perfect Affair, Quercus (2014)

Also by Two Rivers Poets:

David Attwooll, *The Sound Ladder* (2015)
Kate Behrens, *The Beholder* (2012)
Kate Behrens, *Man with Bombe Alaska* (2016)
Adrian Blamires, *The Effect of Coastal Processes* (2005)
Adrian Blamires, *The Pang Valley* (2010)
Adrian Blamires & Peter Robinson (eds.), *The Arts of Peace* (2014)
Joseph Butler, *Hearthstone* (2006)
David Cooke, *A Murmuration* (2015)
Terry Cree, *Fruit* (2014)
Jane Draycott and Lesley Saunders, *Christina the Astonishing* (1998)
Jane Draycott, *Tideway* (2002)
John Froy, *Eggshell: A Decorator's Notes* (2007)
A. F. Harrold, *Logic and the Heart* (2004)
A. F. Harrold, *Flood* (2009)
A. F. Harrold, *The Point of Inconvenience* (2013)
Ian House, *Cutting the Quick* (2005)
Ian House, *Nothing's Lost* (2014)
Gill Learner, *The Agister's Experiment* (2011)
Gill Learner, *Chill Factor* (2016)
Mairi MacInnes, *Amazing Memories of Childhood, etc.* (2016)
Tom Phillips, *Recreation Ground* (2012)
John Pilling and Peter Robinson (eds.), *The Rilke of Ruth Speirs:*
   New Poems, Duino Elegies, Sonnets to Orpheus & Others (2015)
Peter Robinson, *English Nettles and Other Poems* (2010)
Peter Robinson (ed.), *Reading Poetry: An Anthology* (2011)
Peter Robinson (ed.), *A Mutual Friend: Poems for Charles Dickens* (2012)
Peter Robinson, *Foreigners, Drunks and Babies: Eleven Stories* (2013)
Lesley Saunders, *Her Leafy Eye* (2009)
Lesley Saunders, *Cloud Camera* (2012)
Susan Utting, *Houses Without Walls* (2006)
Susan Utting, *Fair's Fair* (2012)
Jean Watkins, *Scrimshaw* (2013)

Interference Effects

Claire Dyer

First published in the uk in 2016 by Two Rivers Press
7 Denmark Road, Reading RG1 5PA.
www.tworiverspress.com

© Claire Dyer 2016

The right of the poet to be identified as the author of the work
has been asserted by her in accordance with the Copyright,
Designs and Patents Act of 1988.

All rights reserved. No part of this publication may be reproduced,
stored in or introduced into a retrieval system, or transmitted,
in any form, or by any means (electronic, mechanical, photocopying,
recording or otherwise) without the prior written permission of
the publisher.

ISBN 978-1-909747-22-7

1 2 3 4 5 6 7 8 9

Two Rivers Press is represented in the uk by Inpress Ltd
and distributed by Central Books.

Cover design and illustration by Sally Castle
Text design by Nadja Guggi and typeset in Janson and Parisine

Printed and bound in Great Britain by Imprint Digital, Exeter.

For my children

The wings of the Morpho butterfly reflect incident light in successive layers, leading to interference effects that produce colours which vary with the viewing angle.

Acknowledgements

My thanks to the editors of *Bedford Square*, *7*, Ward Wood Publishing; *The Emma Press Anthology of Dance*, The Emma Press; *Hands and Wings*, White Rat Press; *Ink Sweat & Tears*; *Old Belongings*, University of Reading Creative Arts Anthology 2015; *Origami Warriors*, University of Reading Creative Arts Anthology 2014; *Slants of Light*, Paragram; *Paris Lit Up No* 1; *Prole*; *SOUTH Poetry*; *The Interpreter's House*; *The Rialto*; *The North*; and *Voyages*, a Reading Writers' Anthology, in whose publications some of these poems, or versions of them, have appeared.

My thanks also to the judges and organisers of the Charles Causley Poetry Competition 2015, The Poetry Society Stanza Competition 2015, Torriano Poetry Competition 2015, Bath Poetry Café Short Poem Competition 2015, the Havant Literary Festival Poetry Competition 2014, the Mslexia Women's Poetry Competition 2015 and the Ware Open Poetry Competition 2015 for awarding prizes to 'Trust and the Horse', 'In the Very Dark', One Small Act of Survival', 'In Chinese the Character for Poetry is Made of Two Parts', 'The Memory Cake', 'Night Walk' and 'Triosch'.

The dedication on page 43 is as requested by a winning bidder in the 2014 CLIC Sargent Get In Character auction (www.clicsargent.org.uk).

Contents

Pocket Globe, 1775 | 1
On the Pier | 2
What Lies Within | 3
Harvesting | 4
The Weight of Two Eggs | 5
Queenie | 6
Swimming Lessons | 7
At Sea | 8
On Sand | 9
Calling My Bluff | 10
Uilleann Music | 11
Indications | 12
After 'The Shampoo' | 13
Night Walk | 14
In the Very Dark | 15
Ready or Not | 16
Good Material | 17
Hotel | 18
That Hollywood Thing | 19
The Answer | 20
Details | 21
The Man Who Didn't Finish *The Great Gatsby* | 22
Holes | 23
Thinking of Manatees | 24
Veritas | 25
The Lamentations of Simultaneous Movements | 26
In Chinese the Character for Poetry is Made of Two Parts | 27
By Design | 28
The Best and the Worst of It | 29
All Night and Near | 30
Acts of Intimacy | 31
The Fledgling | 32
Learning *Bird* | 33
What's Left is This | 34
Lost and Found | 35
The Curators' Assistant | 36
The Label Maker | 37

In the Supermarket | 38
One Small Act of Survival | 39
Ways of Falling –I | 40
Ways of Falling – II | 41
The Memory Cake | 42
Sweet Peas | 43
Perspective | 44
Trust and the Horse | 45
The Interference Effect | 46
Don't Tell Me I've Got It Wrong | 47
Afterword 1: No Detail Too Small | 48
Afterword 2: Aubade | 49

Notes | 51

Pocket Globe, 1775

I am fish. Bishop's fish,
tremendous, unabashed.

I am one of the fishhouses' unnumbered fish;
a fugitive from the knife's worn blade.

I am salmon spawning,
thrash and iridescent flash,

blue air trapped
in rings around my mouth.

I am sleepless in the deep,
hunting, a shadow only – am

mere flick of fin, twitch of muscle
in the kelp. My eyes are fathomless.

I am what's known of silence
until I'm caught, netted, trawled;

until I'm hauled and held,
skinned to make a case

for a heart-sized globe,
on which man has drawn

in miniature what's known
of his new world.

My lining's all that's celestial.
I show to you the heavens.

On the Pier

The summer before Mum died Dad took me fishing on the pier.
It mostly rained, my plastic mac crackled
and the air was stitched with salt and gulls
calling, calling, calling.
We bought our lines from a shop on the front,
the twine thick and tangerine in the grey-green water.
The mackerel we caught were slim and firm as rubber.
Look at the patterns on their backs, Dad said, *their white underbellies.*
They twisted on the deck like tinsel,
then stilled, their mouths slack, their unknowable eyes
staring, staring, staring.
We took our haul to the hotel so Chef could cook them in his kitchen.
He laid them stiff and straight as pencils on a blue china platter.
Even then I had to look away when he served them for our supper.

What Lies Within

Like when you're outside and the lights are on
inside churches and whatever faith there is
is fidgeting under the transept window
and you're back with Nan, slipping fifty pence
into the collection box, fanning
the gilt-edged pages of your hymn book;

or when café chairs are stacked
and striped by sunlight behind the railings
of Pizza Express before it opens
and moorhens are splitting the blue water
of a river nearby and a waiter lights up
his first cigarette of the day;

or when there's a row of shaving mirrors
at the barber's, each tilted to an angle
a few degrees different from its neighbour
so there's always another view of the sky,
another view of a woman smiling at something
the someone she's walking with said;

or when, stepping from a taxi, you see
the fizz-torn dazzle of a street lamp
in the buttery yellow of a pavement after rain
and girls' heels chatter as umbrellas
are folded away and a maraschino cherry
gets dropped into a cocktail glass;

or when you dip your hand into a pond
at Kew and the koi flick and
tremble and whittle your fingers
with their cheese-grater teeth and you stare
and stare into the back of their eyes
looking for what lies within.

Harvesting

Think of fields, an afternoon plump with chaff
and rabbits running the silent way rabbits run,
their eyes the marbles we played with at school.

Imagine the farmer; shirtsleeves rolled, skin hot,
grain under his fingernails – reap, winnow –
the sun filling a blind-white sky.

See the youngster after the life-support's switched off,
an ambulance – its blue light dizzying the windows –
waiting for the heart.

Or, sleepless against the dark, think of the unrecoverable days,
the husks we've gathered into wicker baskets,
and left in shop windows for our grandmothers –

wearing headscarves – to murmur over;
and the eggs, picture the countless children,
what love there is in their sowing and wait.

The Weight of Two Eggs

Whatever poise I have is vested
in my feet – pink-stockinged feet –

toes I can feel the rope through,
nails painted with dabs of Revlon Red.

The pole I carry is the length of a double-decker bus.
On a cloud to my right the bearded man

in his deckchair's marking up his credit/debit list
with a turquoise fountain pen –

my sister's sons for our wise grandpas;
three good and Brylcreemed men.

To my left Nan's baking the perfect Victoria sponge:
two eggs per measure of butter, sugar,

flour weighed out on Weylux scales.
Behind me parents are wearing anxious shades

of beige, waiting for my children;
I try to be more patient, with them and those

I didn't have, those gathered in condoms
or leaked along my thighs, who stained the purple sheets.

The instructions say, *Don't look down.* So I don't,
but still I could be toppled

by the skim of a swift's wing,
a kiss on my wrist's soft pulse.

Queenie

Years back my great-grandmother
stepped off the platform at Earl's Court.
She must have timed it perfectly,

her grief for the child they buried at sea
finally too heavy to hold –
Henry Edward had been a rifleman's boy.

Imagine the people watching, the smack-whack
of the box on the water, the wait
for it to list; how his new bones sank,

his new flesh melting like soap.

Years later my children: bloody and glorious;
four sugar bags each on my chest.
I showed them windows,

told them to look out;
like toughened glass their futures
could gleam, be wonderful perhaps.

Imagine the summers, honeycombs of ribs,
femurs lengthening, journeys home
on Tube trains, their blue eyes shining,

them giving up their seats.

Swimming Lessons

At first Saturday mornings
at St Joseph's, too early,
water that made you blue-cold.

Neither of you wearing
water wings; my heart
round in my mouth for the hour,

the texture and weight of stone.
Then community centre pools,
a Quaker school on Thursdays at five,

sometimes cottages by the sea.
I can't recall when I first let go.
Now you slice the waves,

the sun bright on your backs
and down in Kalkan Old Town
the harbour sings with the call to prayer.

At Sea

Fifty-nine days at sea and
supplies are low:
canned goods, conversation, water.

His lips have blistered
so he cannot kiss her
or shout for help, but he

lets her row more often,
trailing his hand over the side
as a lure for dolphins, mermaids, sharks.

The sun has bleached his hair
almost-white, beacon-white she hopes
if anyone else sails near.

Their blue boat creaks, the gunwale
wood's crazy-paved, only
the letters i, y and J remain

from the name, *Liberty Jane*,
and the seabirds they once believed
were sprites have begun

to browse the ocean,
obsidian-eyed,
wings airy with greed.

She'd thought this would be
her element, and his,
but now they're here

they're not mariners,
are neither in nor out of it.
It's the flowers I miss most,

she tells him,
and the quiet line
between land and sky.

On Sand

They'd booked a blue umbrella sky,
her shoelessness a prelude,
the tide is on the cusp.

He says the sea birds are not watching.
She says their other selves are icebergs,
dancing as icebergs do.

I say whoever's playing the soundtrack
must be on the pier built where the picture ends,
that when they waltz her skin's a shade of calico.

The fishing boats aren't yet back –
nets plump with the day's last catch.

A man on the quay is whistling
as he shuts the shutters of his shop.

Calling My Bluff

after Jen Hadfield

Triosch, *noun*: the precise shade of blue an emergency vehicle's light bar throws onto the underside of bridges or motorway flyovers at night; the sound small waves drawing back through shingle make when you're barefoot and the sky's patterned like snakeskin and the air soft as muslin; the moment the rain stops and the silence is louder than heartbeats; the finger-nail-thin split in the skin of a tomato that's stayed too long on the vine; the breathing of babies when they sleep and their limbs are starfished on cool sheets; a woman unable to face an uncomfortable truth who has a penchant for sand and remote sandy places.

Uilleann Music

A crowd. We wait;
stage lights warming
through like hands,

celebration and *solace*
in our laps. It is
November outside.

Then, the grace notes
bring summer back:
that blue rug from the car,

bomber bees,
Camembert, Chianti,
your blithe laughter,

our bodies deftly able;
they bring the fleet beat
of babies' hearts,

the soft shadows
of children in
rhododendron woods –

their castles, roadways
and imagined cities;
bring how heat lifts dust

from wheat fields
to blind us, coat
lips meant for kissing.

Indications

A slate-skyed morning,
an afternoon fat with rain
or more likely, dark outside,

and cold – frost like sugar
icing the Lexus
you've recently bought,

the hands you've blown on
with your just-kissed-me mouth
clamped to the steering wheel

as you drive away.
The idea is simple,
is about touch and skin,

half-open lips, our bodies' vocabulary
while the furniture stays silent.
It's not supposed to be

you turning at the lights,
coming back to lamp glow,
the pattern I stare at on the bedroom carpet

to stop the clock.
We're supposed to be
better at this than that.

After 'The Shampoo'

I'd read Bishop; that night
dreamt we were outside the cinema,
you washing my hair
with coconut-scented shampoo,
with strangers watching us
and the fat man on the steps
playing an edgy kind of jazz.

The air was tropical,
soap-softened water damped
the blue collar of my dress,
each droplet burrowed and,
where it touched skin, flowered
into celandines until
there was a garden of them
between my breasts.

Your fingers were extraordinary
– I'd closed my eyes by then
but somehow knew
you were studying
my bowed head as if
I was a minnow hooked
on a line of catgut perhaps.

Your neck is beautiful, you said
so quietly I almost didn't hear.

Night Walk

Being sleepless I take my faults for a walk.
I'm also carrying five purple alliums
and sometimes it rains.

The path I follow borders a maize field,
a duvet of lapwings rises from it
crying *pee-wit, wit, wit-eeze, wit.*

In another field a tractor is harrowing
what I should have left unspoken,
the soil is walnut-brown, and

nearby a copse hides what I should have said
instead; I hear my sentences stepping through
the elms with the caution of deer.

A sea wind dimples a distant sea,
bothered by gulls, gritty as Spitfires.
Next, a cairn: each stone a worry.

I lay the alliums down as homage,
reach out my hand, already know the stones
for their stone wildness, their necessary weight.

In the Very Dark

In the very dark of the night it rained,
a fall of sudden and surprising rain
sounding like the sea or snap of sheets
shaken out for the line.

I lay and listened to its roar,
now sheet, now ocean roar,
with a dream of mirrors spooling in my head,
flickering the way home movies do,

so nothing was real and yet everything was;
on the screen saw Balmedie Beach and you,
in blue, arms out, head thrown back
and waiting for the rain,

knew then the second's pause before it came
had always been the joy itself, not just a link between.

Ready or Not

In the garden my children cover their eyes
and the counting begins like our grandmothers said.
Time hides in the hawthorn to muffle its cries,

it hears the trees moan, their sorrowful sighs
and its sad heart softens with words from the dead.
In the garden my children cover their eyes.

No one believes that forever will fill in the skies,
scribble them ribbons of blue and red –
time hides in the hawthorn to muffle its cries.

It rewrites our stories with promises, lies;
keeps a leather-bound book of them under its bed.
In the garden my children cover their eyes,

the words *Coming to get you* in the dark of their minds.
They look over their shoulders, their shoes made of lead;
time hides in the hawthorn to muffle its cries.

But it finds us at last; it sings as it flies,
chants *Ready or not*, like our grandmothers said.
In the garden my children cover their eyes,
time hides in the hawthorn to muffle its cries.

Good Material

Say we're in a mall, the floor's glittery,
flecked with talking, somewhat dazzling.

> Midnight, a rooftop bar, air all warm,
> wild celery – your hands are mostly ready.

> Or Starbucks, our names in black marker on the cups,
> you tapping a wooden stirrer on the table.

Say it's dark, you're tired from driving,
your shirt smells of cinnamon and the ocean's

> an absence, but there's sea salt on our skin.

Or a train, wine a history in our mouths,
your coat is thick and navy.

> Say it's a hotel room, time is bruiseful
> yet you're sleeping.

Say it's over, I unzip your spine, let in the light,
pick at your ribs, sift through the gleanings.

Hotel

I want furniture more lasting than itself,
for it to speak of 1910,

a weekend shooting party before the world went tilt,
footsteps on the stairs – polished wood

like conker sheen – Willow pattern, kitchen
steam, a skinned rabbit in the scullery.

I want music in the ballroom, my grandmother's furs,
menthol cigarette, paste ring, a grandfather's

smile; want the orchestra to play in cornices
and balustrades, for there to be beads of spit

in the oboist's reed, a conductor beating time.

*

It's always the window first,
an incalculable sky.

Check-in was surrender,
and now we're held by curtains that don't fit,

the theatre of tap drip, a ceiling fan
moving air in languages we don't know.

Your jacket's on the chair and
afterwards we always leave

part of what we want to keep.

That Hollywood Thing

Next day I did that Hollywood thing –
corny I know – as if New England

was outside the window, not London
and an unconvincing sky, the Thames nearby,

still inky, blue with last night's leftover dark;
as if I had an audience and Mantovani

was playing and this wasn't Friday
in Trafalgar Square, the pavements dry,

commuters commuting in slow motion,
the coffee shops already full; as if the camera

panned to a seashore, to some crabs skittering,
sunlight ambering their backs, the answer

to this tucked under their shells, the music
now at its end notes and those in their seats

preparing to leave; so, as if it would make
any difference, I placed my hand on the pillow

where your head should have been
and spread my fingers wide,

said *Wish you were here* without
moving my lips, then made my way to the door;

the last shot would be of it closing
with its hotel-type *whoomp-click*

and we'd all be left staring
at implacable wood as *The End*

appeared as a screen shot
and the credits started to roll.

The Answer

In these heartlands
my need-to-know scalds
my teeth when we kiss.

So I journey to the borderlands
where the answer sits
sagely in its castle built

from marble, figs, white Zinfandel.
Here, leaves lift each October
to green the trees, form buds

that glisten. Here, skin fades
in the sun; the dead un-die,
put on clothes we've given away

and skylines flatten, blue light
shines off bright windows as
workers dismantle steel frames,

tip earth into foundation holes,
children unlearn our story,
their limbs soften to embryos.

Details

Flood waters cover the towpath, the plains up to the road.

A drift of swans by the steps to the boathouse.

The Thames is electroplated,
the sun pale, low in a solid sky.

A woman throws a blue ball for her dog,
it runs the shallows, the sound like hooves galloping.

Birdsong dissolves the air and in the trees:
old nests, ground ivy, a thousand slanting shadows.

The tight buds glisten.

Further away the geese let the currents take them,
then rise, an applause of wings and necks that ripple.

The wind woodpeckers a streetlamp.

After a while, we drive home.

The Man Who Didn't Finish
The Great Gatsby

The man who didn't finish *The Great Gatsby*
had a flat tyre on the North Circular

when it was evening and quietly raining.
Maybe he was on his way home from work,

or to a house where she was waiting.
(It's possible he'd read of the *men and girls*

who *came and went like moths* out loud
last time they met, her head warm

on his shoulder.) Maybe he'd bought groceries –
steak perhaps, wine, a bunch of English asparagus,

it being late May when lawns are blue
and the air moves like music,

that he'd paid for in cash and lifted out of the boot
so he could reach the jack and spare,

the book perched in a bag on the pavement,
the edges of its pages starting to curl

and, when the wheel was fixed, his hands
wiped clean on a rag, it had gone,

so he drove on, chose not to finish, but stop
there, then, as though someone had put out a light.

Holes

Each road has purpose but
when men in Hi-Vis jackets,
hard hats and safety boots
dig up the corner of Vigo Street,
its particular imperative stops.

There are no taxi cabs, buses,
cars, no couriers on blue motorbikes
with family photos taped
inside their windshields
next to maps of Mayfair,

just people on pavements,
quiet among the jackhammers
and JCBs and it's about detours,
holes. And, in these holes I see
layers of aggregate, think

of drainage – into one
someone's thrown an empty
cigarette packet, its white
luminous against the dirt.
I know why they're here,

these men in their Hi-Vis coats.
They must be searching where you stood
for the slender fissures,
the catastrophic fault lines
you made when you chose

to side-step, walk away.

Thinking of Manatees

And when the thunder comes I think
of the Everglades and manatees,
how boat propellers bite

chunks out of them leaving
teeth marks like in apples,
and when the thunder comes

it rolls insistent in its purpleness,
making sounds like release,
like sex does, and when

the thunder comes I watch blue clouds
collide, banks of them soldered
by lightning, by the fall of rain

and how car tyres slick the road,
and I remember you, the shape of you
naked in front of the mirror

as you checked your phone,
your head bent and
the lamplight bright on it.

Veritas

I call you from bars when it's evening
and the music's not reaching
the corners. I call you from trains

when it's raining and the rain's
plastic on the windows and the fields
are fading away. I call you from cities –

packed with cars bleating;
and from headlands, where the sea
draws back and is waiting

as the line rings, as it rings. I call you
at night with the scent of fox sharp
in my garden and the moon plump, blue

and ready to fall. And say just once
you pick up, ask how I am. How am I?
I'll say, *I'm OK, it's OK, I don't miss you at all.*

The Lamentations of Simultaneous Movements

Say I touch my face and in another world you touch yours.
What follows is a sort of keening.

> Somewhere a sun is glinting, the sky's cross-stitched
> with wind and wire and we are puppets.

Say I turn to face the water, there is wailing as you do the same.
Shadows rend the air,

> skim the ocean; the wash they leave behind is salty-
> blue. In both our places we are riven.

Say we learn to fly, soar high on thermals, hands cupped to our ears,
fugitives from separation.

> What follows will be hush, the banshees' surrender;
> their doeskin bags packed tight with raw laments.

In Chinese the Character for Poetry is Made of Two Parts

Word 言
Outside the door she pauses
to take off her shoes, cover her head.

The steps are marbled by the sun,
are cold. She genuflects,

the light's beaded.
All around is gold.

If someone were watching
they would see his name in her shoulders

threaded under the skin, blue
like capillaries are blue, and howling.

Temple 寺
Later at a bureau inlaid with ebony,
mother of pearl – the day's heat

a sound in the wood –
she takes parchment.

The stays in her corset are his fingers;
her hair's coiled at her nape, and heavy.

Outside are hummingbirds,
maple trees. The ink blot's

not for Rorschach, it reads
Worship. If someone were watching.

By Design

They set the stage with clocks
made languorous like limbs after love.

Behind me a plumber sits on his haunches
watching time drip faultlessly

and smiling while the Best Boy,
having filled tinfoil troughs

with water a hundred shades of blue,
shines a torch on the papier-mâché cliffs

and someone says, *The tree's keeping time
at arm's length, we made the lashes*

*of the whatever-it-is out of horsehair
and coated the gold case with honey,*

sent invites to the ants in yesterday's post.
I see the seven o'clock fly lick his lips,

slip off my shoes, get ready to step up.
Once there I'll know for sure that all

is and will be artificial by design,
for now and for ever more.

The Best and the Worst of It

More happened that year
than the worst of it:

in the National Gallery
Mary Richardson

took a meat cleaver to a Velázquez,
Shaw's *Pygmalion* hit the stage,

Joseph Chamberlain died and
the first colour feature film

played in a picture house
when *The Times* cost a penny

and lads stretched out their legs,
shared bags of humbugs with their girls.

And, above a tailor's shop in Bethnal Green
Dora's mother boiled water,

readied towels for the boy born blue,
the cord around his neck

while his father went to war.
They named him Alfie, this boy

who'd never know the best of it
or any of it at all.

All Night and Near

the North Sea is panther-black –
his sleek dark haunches.

All night and near his pianist's claws
strafe the shingle,

his blue lips foam,
the moon yellow in his eyes

and oh, I know he desires me, that
come morning

mad gulls will shred the sky as I reach land,
his saliva will bead my thighs.

Acts of Intimacy

Barely remembered
but like the light that hangs from

streetlamps in fog it is faint,
a pulse yellowing the night,

bringing back before
when we held all we had, and you

were close with notes and beats and rhythms,
with sureness and the ease of it.

Your breath is on my neck
somewhere still

as these pale blue hours inch to morning and I,
words dressed up as kisses in my mouth,

learn how poems can impersonate
a body that's intimate and infinite.

The Fledgling

I didn't really want it.
It came during that last call
when you said *I've been thinking*

and I heard a sound
like fabric tearing –
the old woman must be making

birds from bits of cloth again,
her shoulders bent,
her ten discoloured fingernails.

It moved in; small, fluttery,
beady-eyed. I flapped at it
with spatulas, odd bits of laundry,

sometimes sad songs on the radio.
Last week it must have flown
too high because it fell

blue as rain into the glass vase
I carry around with me.
Maybe it'll reduce,

become a second heart
beating a fraction
out of time with the first.

Of course, it'll be frailer,
more afraid, lilac, veined,
the size of a quail's egg.

Maybe if I keep it warm.

Learning *Bird*

I'm learning *Bird* at night school.
Our teacher's a raven with kind eyes.
The classroom is up three flights of stairs and
to our west the Thames shines
like blue aluminium in this late-summer light.
Some nights necklaces of geese fly over us.
I imagine my pulse in their wings,
imagine the air they leave in their wake
is threaded with pearls.
This week we're learning *Chaffinch*:
all its frill and torrent.
The raven tells us we must be joyful,
we must open our throats,
throw back our heads to release the song.

What's Left is This

Then, by the cashpoint
inside Lloyds Bank a man
in a blue coat takes
my collar bone, plucks

it straight out. I'm surprised
it doesn't hurt.
Standing in line at Tesco's,
basket at my feet –

pack of waterproof plasters,
jar of olives, two pears –
a woman with red hair
whips out my left hip.

I'm a bit off kilter now,
reckon we should move on,
to my organs perhaps.
At lunch I offer the waiter a lung.

He's from Melbourne he says,
just passing through,
but accepts it anyhow –
a few drops of blood

on the wooden floor,
nothing more. And
what's left is this – some ribs,
a voice, one marvellous heart.

Lost and Found

I think I left it by the till
next to the two-for-ones.

It was with me when I set out;
I remember its stone-weight,

probably had to juggle it a bit
getting in the car, put it

on the passenger seat where
it may have left a mark.

But by the precinct tree
that's weeping leaves

now autumn's here, I find
I'm empty-handed, porous,

bereft, so retrace my steps
past the tables outside Costa, past

some dogs asleep at their owners' heels,
litter that's jitter-bugging sadly

and the remains of cigarettes
in blue plastic ashtrays.

Outside the supermarket
I look amongst the trolleys' wheels.

Naturally, it's not there.
Instead I find it by the till

next to the two-for-ones
flapping in a dying fish sort of way.

So you see in the end I was right.

The Curators' Assistant

Say he had a job in the City once, travelled in on the 6.02,
his lifetime's grail to find words to capture
                              the full palette of the sky.

Now I work nights with him here and sometimes
when we place pieces on white shelves,

hang pictures on blue walls he rests his hands on mine.
The hours pass slowly,

the quiet bespoke and reverential so that when we speak
we speak in whispers until our displays are done.

Tonight it's the *Head of a Laughing Child*
                              from the Chelsea Factory
(in slip-cast soft-paste porcelain on loan
                              from a private collection);

it's *netsuke* and a filigree perfume case and stand
                              in Chinese silver,
an engraving on ivory so intricate its beauty can only be seen

through the lens of a magnifying glass;
it's Number 11 in the case by the door –

a tin-glazed earthenware *Dish* dated 1526
from Castel Durante or Venice, no one is totally sure.

We'll make a gift of these for tomorrow's people
then put our gloves away.

We'll say goodbye and I'll walk home in the heron-wing
                              grey of morning,
get into bed beside you, match my breath to your breathing,
give back my heart for safe-keeping.

The Label Maker

has small hands,
can stitch hummingbird-quick,

favours wearing bright colours:
lime, cerise, aquamarine.

He carries a pop-up house in a velveteen bag,
is bald, shameless, has obsidian eyes.

See him wait outside M&S for the man to sit,
bend his head; see the coins,

the wire-haired dog. See the Label Maker's
cotton of heron-wing grey,

the label says *Homeless*.
See him follow a woman to a hotel door,

watch as she checks in.
He leans against a wall, stitches

her *Faithless* with silver thread.
See him at the chemist's with fabric on his lap

as the boy who once was loved
swallows methadone, hands back the plastic cup.

The word now is *Hopeless*.
See him in your kitchen.

See your child. On the table
is a form for something ordinary.

See him make ready when they falter
at the gender box.

See the sun glint on his needle and his small hands.
See your honeycomb heart shatter, fall.

In the Supermarket

The girl in the supermarket picks up a Gala melon,
holds it in both of her hands.
It's late, she's tired, it's been a bitch of a day.
She notices the boy stacking apples:
his blue shirt, tattoo, nails bitten down to the quick.
The lights are hot on her back,
outside it's that-night-dark, the hospital one
when she'd looked out at the town's
headlamps and streetlamps and the load
in her belly had been mighty.
Her baby had the most beautiful eyes.
There are pains in her lungs, in the fist of her heart,
her muscles ache like a long-distance runner's;
she can feel the fell stones shift under her feet.

One Small Act of Survival

In my hand a shiny new hammer
bought to forge a carapace from commonplace things:

door handles, empty soup cans, the almost-over
hyacinth blooms in my mother's blue vase.

The shape I'll fashion will not be symmetrical
but I'll spend a while writing charms on its underside

then flip it, polish its surface until I can see my face in it.
It'll be shallow, and roughly the size of silence.

Next up, a Stanley knife to incise my chest,
                                    peel back the skin.
My blood will blossom like chrysanthemums
                                          as I slide my creation in.

Ways of Falling – I

Age five and slipping off the blue metal swing
                               out back at 13 Marlyns Drive,
it was a given the soil would be concrete-hard,
                               Copydex'd with dead grass.

The friction of my hands tripping down the chains
                               lifted the scent
of hot offal into the air and made the sound of trains, and

landing, I stared up at swing's A frame, made pictures
                               from its acne of rust
as layers of earth travelled through my bones. I vomited

them out of my mouth in a shower of magma and stones,
could not move and was, it seemed, thigh-deep
                               in lava and shingle,

a savoy cabbage planted in my chest with a detonator inside.
I remember counting while waiting for the tingle,
                               for it to explode.

Ways of Falling – II

Now I fish in the back room of my house
                              and count and wait.
There is friction and track-rattle and I brace,
                              but it's a given

each word will struggle and flail. Sometimes
the sun thwacks against their scales, there's a hint
                              of phosphorescence

and their mouths gape as I lift them clear,
my line hooked hard in their soft fish lips.
                              I watch them

slap the dry grasses, their fish slime drying slowly,
marble eyes watching a Tuesday-blue sky as I count
                              and wait for them to die.

Sometimes sirens sound on London Road, there's always a little blood
and it me who falls backwards and the ground cracks daily,
                              the ground cracks daily.

The Memory Cake

When I was seven my mother baked a memory cake.
First into the bowl was the ribbed white blanket
                              from her hospital bed.
Next, her final journey home.
Then she blended my forget-me-not dress
                              and its smocking and pockets
with the snip-snackle-crack of the windbreak
                              that day on the sands,
and how she said *Here comes the cavalry* at the end of films,
and I'd see horses tossing their heads, desert dust
                              rising in clouds.
Next she added story times, the ice-cream van's jingle-twang,
sunshine that fell slow on my back
the morning we got up early to check if the fledglings had flown.
I watched her beat the mix, fold in her smile,
her hands moving all the while like mine and, when it was done
she left it to cool on the counter top, said *Make sure you eat it slowly,
crumb by crumb* as, outside the window, some rain began to fall.

Sweet Peas

for Vivien Tottle

Sweet peas. My grandfather.
The two always linked

in some strange way.
His bulk. Their fragility –

flowers balanced like butterflies feeding.
Mornings we'd walk beside the wigwam canes,

dew between my toes,
him knowing answers to questions I didn't ask

and we'd pick fresh stems for Nan,
for her kitchen table under its window

with its blue-painted sill,
the souvenir from Oberammergau

between two potted plants.
The sweet peas would tremble

as we sat down to eat, some sun
still in Grandpa's Brylcreemed hair.

There are times, small and unremarkable times,
when I wonder what I'll be remembered for:

one flower, one morning,
one particular look

across a room
as some rain begins to fall.

Perspective

Before I knew you only
had two months left,
I wanted not an idea of beauty,

but the blade of beauty against my throat,
wanted a bone handle, chamfered
steel, blood's insistence;

wanted a child on a beach
reaching out a hand
to touch the sun the way kids do

when they believe it'll fit
inside their palm; wanted
a cormorant's blue-black back

arrowing the foam and rising,
its yellow eyes brilliant,
its yellow eyes brilliant coins of triumph;

wanted the bird to swallow its catch,
the awful spasm of muscle and gullet;
wanted the bird's easy flight

to where the child's hand pointed;
wanted to be captivated by this,
to balance my body on a knife's edge.

Trust and the Horse

'Always it is by bridges that we live.' —*Philip Larkin*

One day I will ride to the poem on horseback.
The poem will be far away, built

from the spaces between lines and wires,
from words made with the voices of birds.

My horse will sway, his coat
dusty with heat and the company of flies;

his head will nod with a wisdom and rhythm
that's hypnotic, powerful, blind. The bridge

we'll cross will be of hope and oak,
echoes and orphans will live in the shadows beneath.

And below us will be water and sometimes sand.
And below us will sometimes be sky.

What I fear is trust, but my horse will step surely
in the daylight and the nightlight.

My horse will step to the pop of fish breath
and the shudder of shorelines.

My horse will step through blue air.
My horse and I will step together,

will measure our footfalls
in millions and in small numbers.

The Interference Effect

As with the Morpho's wing
it depends on the angle:

in the photograph we're laughing,
he's wearing his blue sweater,
his arms around me, loosely;

there are the flowers in the curtains
the sun turned lemon yellow
those afternoons we played hooky,

ate toast in bed, and, afterwards,
slept the way we slept,
his arms around me, loosely;

and there's the night
next to the slow water of the lake
when we melted snow on our tongues,

time snug in our pockets,
wrapped up in ticket stubs,
his arms still around me, loosely.

I move my head and the picture changes;
layer upon layer the colours loosen
until they too slip out of shot

and always and forever's gone by
and I look and look and look
until there's nothing left to see.

Don't Tell Me I've Got It Wrong

It was hot,
heat rising from the roofs of cars,

heat solid and surprising
that made warm the pavements and the walls.

The summer leaves moved soundlessly.
The sky was blue like Morpho butterflies are blue.

And, at the market there was you,
buying apples in a shirt the green of apples.

Your eyes were otter-brown and
I stood next to you,

looked down as you turned around,
four apples in a bag in your hand.

Love, you said and I knew you'd picked me too,
that, in time, your flesh would leave its mark on mine,

like stitches or like sunburn
when lovers spend good times by the sea.

So, don't tell me I've got it wrong:
I felt your apple breath,

the heat, the green heat of your shirt
when it was hot;

heat solid and surprising that rose
from the roofs of cars, made warm the pavements

and the walls that day the sky was blue like Morpho butterflies
are blue and you saw me, I saw you.

Afterword 1: No Detail Too Small

Cento after Elizabeth Bishop

These peninsulas take the water between thumb and finger.
At low tide like this how sheer the water is.
The air smells so strong of codfish.
Black-and-white man-of-war birds soar
on impalpable drafts
and open their tails like scissors on the curves
or tense them like wishbones, till they tremble.
                The light
grows richer; the fog,
shifting, salty, thin,
comes closing in.
Here comes that old man with the stick and sack,
meandering again.
There are sequins on his vest and on his thumb.
There is a fence of chicken wire along the dock.
                Oil has seeped into
the margins of the ditch of standing water
and flashes or looks up brokenly,
like bits of mirror – no, more blue than that:
like tatters of the *Morpho* butterfly.
If lightning struck the house now, it would run
from the four blue china balls on top.
It is marvellous to wake up together.
The world might change to something quite different.
The beach hisses like fat.
The millions of grains are black, white, tan, and gray,
mixed with quartz, rose and amethyst.

Afterword 2: Aubade

I wear your breath like wool,
the sheets are warm and

you're faltering by the door
so, before you leave, I read you

the poem of your going;
the poem is your shoes,

your car, our neighbours' kids
on their way to school,

it is itself and something other,
this version of us: these

bodies, this space; each comma
a present and remembered kiss;

the poem follows you;
on the roof of number 9

builders are cut-outs
against the sky; we watch you

drive away and I read
to keep you where I've written us,

where we're sleeping,
all this still in the making.

'Language is like shot silk; so much depends on the angle at which it is held.'
—*The French Lieutenant's Woman*, John Fowles

Notes

'Pocket Globe, 1775' – as seen in the Ashmolean Museum, Oxford.

'On Sand' – after *The Singing Butler* by Jack Vettriano.

'Uilleann Music' – after *A Tribute to Seamus Heaney*, Southbank Centre, 20 November 2013.

'By Design' – after *The Persistence of Memory* by Salvador Dalí.

'The Curators' Assistant' – The Holburne Museum, Bath.

'The Interference Effect' & 'Don't Tell Me I've Got It Wrong' – after 'Under the Window: Ouro Prêto', in *Elizabeth Bishop: Complete Poems*, Chatto & Windus, London, 2004.

'No Detail Too Small' – with lines (all by Elizabeth Bishop) from:
'The Map', *North & South*, 1946;
'The Bight' and 'At the Fishhouses', *A Cold Spring*, 1955;
'Sandpiper', *Questions of Travel*, 1965;
'The Moose', *Geography III*, 1976;
'Under the Window: Ouro Prêto', Uncollected, *Elizabeth Bishop: Complete Poems*.
'It is Marvellous to Wake up Together...', Uncollected.

John Fowles quote from *The French Lieutenant's Woman*, Vintage (Penguin Random House) 2004.

Two Rivers Press has been publishing in and about Reading since 1994. Founded by the artist Peter Hay (1951–2003), the press continues to delight readers, local and further afield, with its varied list of individually designed, thought-provoking books.